NA1
AMALFI COAST
TRAVEL GUIDE
2025

**Your Ultimate Planner for Italy's
Best Coastal Villages, Foodie
Hotspots, Insider Tips and
Historical Treasures**

Albert S. Swim

Copyright © 2025 (Albert S. Swim)

DISCLAIMER

Welcome to the *Naples and Amalfi Coast Travel Guide 2025*, your gateway to exploring the enchanting allure of southern Italy, where ancient history meets breathtaking coastal vistas. From lively Naples and its world-renowned cuisine to the sun-drenched villages of the Amalfi Coast, this region offers a feast for the senses and a journey through culture, beauty, and tradition.

Please note: While every effort has been made to provide accurate and up-to-date information, the dynamic nature of travel means that conditions, access, and services can change without notice. Seasonal variations, local regulations, and unforeseen circumstances may impact your experience. Always check with local authorities, tourism offices, or trusted experts before embarking on your adventures to ensure a safe and enjoyable trip.

Table Of Contents

4

OVERALL MAP

Naples

☐Vesuvius

☐Herculaneum

☐Pompeii

Gulf of Naples

Salerno

Ravello

Furore

Positano

Sorrento

Praiano   Amalfi

Capri

Amalfi Coast

Introduction

Naples and **the Amalfi Coast**, you've stolen my heart once again! Every time I visit, it feels like falling in love all over, but 2025 promises to be something truly extraordinary. This year, the magic of southern Italy seems to be calling louder than ever, and I can't wait to share it all with you.

Landing in **Naples**, I was swept away by the city's incredible energy. It's a place where every street hums with life, every corner reveals a story, and every meal feels like a celebration. Wandering through the bustling markets, I found myself captivated by the vibrant colors of fresh produce, the irresistible aromas of street food, and the joyful sounds of locals going about their day. Naples is a feast for the senses, a city that pulls you in and refuses to let go.

Next, I set off along the **Amalfi Coast**, and let me tell you—this place is a dream come true. Imagine winding coastal roads with views so stunning they make you gasp, pastel-hued villages cascading down cliffs, and the sparkling Mediterranean stretching endlessly before you. It's like stepping into a painting, only better, because you're living it.

In **Positano**, I strolled along charming cobblestone streets lined with boutique shops and fragrant lemon groves. Amalfi welcomed me with its majestic cathedral and a warm sea breeze that carried the promise of endless relaxation. Ravello stole my breath with its lush gardens and panoramic views that seemed to stretch to forever. Each stop along the way felt like discovering a new piece of paradise.

And the food? Oh, the food! From savoring fresh seafood at a seaside trattoria to indulging in creamy gelato as the sun dipped below the horizon, every bite was a revelation. The tang of **Amalfi lemons**, the richness of handmade pasta, the crisp perfection of a chilled glass of local wine—it was a culinary journey I'll never forget.

But the real magic was in the moments: watching the sunset cast golden hues over the **Tyrrhenian Sea**, feeling the warmth of the sun on my face as I hiked the Path of the Gods, and sharing stories with locals who welcomed me like family. These experiences, these connections, are what make Naples and the Amalfi Coast so unforgettable.

Leaving this region always feels bittersweet. It's not just a place; it's a feeling—a vibrant, life-affirming energy that stays with you long after you've left. The landscapes, the people, the culture—they remind you to slow down, savor every moment, and embrace the beauty all around you.

So, if you've been dreaming of **Naples** and **the Amalfi Coast**, let this be your sign to make it happen. Pack your bags, step into the magic, and prepare for an adventure that will touch your heart and inspire your soul. You'll leave with incredible memories, a deeper appreciation for life, and maybe even a little piece of this enchanting region to carry with you always.

Naples and the Amalfi Coast are waiting for you, my friend.

Chapter 1: Welcome to Naples and Amalfi Coast

A. A Brief History

Naples and the Amalfi Coast are not just destinations—they're stories written in stone, sea, and culture. Their histories stretch back thousands of years, shaping the beautiful places we see today.

Naples, or *Napoli* as the locals call it, is one of the oldest continuously inhabited cities in the world. It was founded by the Greeks in the 8th century BC and named *Neapolis*, which means **"New City."** From the start, Naples was a hub of activity. Its location near the Bay of Naples made it a natural meeting point for traders, explorers, and settlers. Over the centuries, the city came under the control of the Romans, who expanded it into a bustling center of culture and commerce. Even today, you can feel the echoes of those times when you walk through its historic streets.

But history wasn't always kind to Naples. The city faced invasions, plagues, and natural disasters, including the eruption of **Mount Vesuvius** in AD 79 that buried nearby Pompeii and Herculaneum. Despite the challenges, Naples endured, and each new wave of rulers—Byzantines, Normans, Spanish, and French—left their mark. These influences created a city with a unique personality: bold, chaotic, and unapologetically passionate.

While Naples flourished on land, the Amalfi Coast grew into a maritime powerhouse. During the Middle Ages, the Republic of Amalfi was one of Italy's most important seafaring states. Its sailors and merchants traded goods like spices, silk, and gold across the Mediterranean and beyond. Amalfi even developed its own set of maritime laws, known as **the** *Amalfitan Code*, which influenced shipping for centuries.

The Amalfi Coast's villages—Positano, Ravello, and others—also have their own rich histories. Many of these settlements date back to Roman times, and you can still see evidence of ancient villas tucked into the cliffs. Over time, the steep terrain forced locals to become resourceful, creating terraced farms to grow lemons, olives, and grapes. These traditions continue today, giving the Amalfi Coast its signature charm.

The **Renaissance** brought an explosion of art and architecture to both Naples and the Amalfi Coast. In Naples, grand churches like the Naples Cathedral and lavish palaces were built, reflecting the wealth and power of the city's elite. Meanwhile, Ravello became a retreat for artists and thinkers, with its famous gardens like Villa Cimbrone inspiring creativity for centuries.

In modern times, both Naples and the Amalfi Coast have become icons of Italian culture. Naples is the birthplace of **pizza**, a culinary treasure beloved around the world. The Amalfi Coast, with its stunning cliffs and sparkling seas, has captured the hearts of travelers, writers, and filmmakers.

What makes this region so special is how its history is still alive today. Walking through Naples' chaotic streets, you feel the energy of generations who've lived there. Along the Amalfi Coast, the traditions of fishing, farming, and hospitality continue as they have for centuries.

B.Key Facts

Let me set the stage for you—Naples and the Amalfi Coast are two of the most fascinating and breathtaking places you'll ever visit. Before you pack your bags, let's go over some key facts to help you feel right at home when you arrive. Don't worry, I'll keep it simple and straightforward—just like a friend sharing tips

1.Where Exactly Are We Going?

Naples and the Amalfi Coast are in southern Italy, in the Campania region. Think warm weather, incredible food, and views that will make your jaw drop. Naples is your gateway city, buzzing with life, culture, and history. From there, it's a quick journey to the Amalfi Coast, where you'll find picturesque villages clinging to cliffs above the dazzling Tyrrhenian Sea.

Here's a tip: Make sure your camera or phone has plenty of storage—you're going to need it.

2.UNESCO World Heritage Wonders

This isn't just any old region—it's recognized as a UNESCO World Heritage site for good reason. Naples' historic center is a treasure trove of ancient ruins, baroque architecture, and bustling markets that make you feel like you've stepped into a living history book. Over on the Amalfi Coast, the combination of natural beauty and centuries-old villages is nothing short of magical. Every street, every turn, tells a story. You'll feel like you're walking through a postcard.

3.Language and Currency—The Essentials

Okay, here's the deal: The official language is Italian, but don't stress. In tourist-heavy areas like Naples and the Amalfi Coast, many locals speak English. Still, learning a few basic phrases like *Ciao* (hello), *Grazie* (thank you), and *Per favor* (please) will go a long way and earn you some smiles.

The currency is the Euro (€). Credit cards are widely accepted, but having some cash is smart for small purchases, especially if you're grabbing a quick espresso or a gelato at a local café. And trust me, you'll want to do both. Often.

4.What's So Special About This Place?

Naples is the birthplace of pizza. Need I say more? This city has a heart and soul that you'll feel in every bite, every historic alley, and every conversation. On the Amalfi Coast, you'll find the kind of beauty that makes you pause and take a deep breath. Lemon groves, pastel-colored villages, and sunsets that look like they were painted just for you.

5.Getting Around

In Naples, you've got plenty of options: the metro, buses, and taxis all make getting around easy. When you head to the Amalfi Coast, things slow down—ferries, buses, and even walking become part of the experience. If you're driving, remember that those coastal roads are as thrilling as they are narrow. Just take it slow and enjoy the ride—or let someone else do the driving while you soak in the views.

C.How to Use This Guide

Welcome! You've got the *Naples and Amalfi Coast Travel Guide 2025* in your hands, and I'm so excited to be your travel buddy on this journey. Think of this guide as your personal roadmap, helping you navigate through two of Italy's most beautiful and exciting regions.

What You'll Find in This Guide

Let's break it down. This guide is packed with practical information, insider tips, and plenty of inspiration to make planning as easy and fun as possible.

Here's a quick overview:

1. **Getting Started**
   o The early chapters are all about setting the stage: why Naples and the Amalfi Coast are must-visit destinations, what makes 2025 special, and key details like the best time to visit and how to get

there. It's everything you need to get excited about your trip.

2. **Deep Dives into Each Destination**
   ○ You'll find dedicated sections for Naples and each major stop along the Amalfi Coast—Positano, Amalfi, Ravello, and more. These chapters cover top attractions, must-try foods, hidden gems, and the vibe of each location so you know exactly what to expect.

3. **Practical Tips**
   ○ This guide is also your go-to for logistics. Need to know how to get around? Want to avoid tourist traps? Curious about cultural etiquette? I've got you covered.

4. **Itineraries**
   ○ If you're not sure how to organize your trip, don't worry. I've included sample itineraries for different time frames, from quick 3-day trips to longer 7-day adventures. Use them as-is or customize them to suit your style.

How to Use It While Planning

Think of this guide as your pre-trip best friend. Start with the sections that catch your eye—maybe you're curious about Naples' historic center or the best beaches on the Amalfi Coast. Jot down the spots that excite you most, and then move on to the itineraries to see how they fit into your schedule.

Make sure to check out the practical tips for things like transportation and accommodations. These sections will save you time, money, and stress when you're on the ground.

How to Use It on the Ground

When you're actually in Naples or the Amalfi Coast, this guide will still have your back. Treat it like your pocket expert, ready to help you find the best pizza spot, a hidden hiking trail, or a quick escape from the crowds. Use the maps, tips, and recommendations to explore with confidence.

One pro tip? Stay flexible! Plans might shift (and that's okay). Some of the best travel moments happen when you wander off the beaten path or stumble across something unexpected.

Chapter 2: Getting There and Around

A. How to Reach Naples and Amalfi

By Air

Planning your dream trip to Naples and the enchanting Amalfi Coast in 2025? Let's make your journey as smooth as possible by exploring the best ways to get there by air.

Major Airports Serving the Region

1. **Naples International Airport (Aeroporto di Napoli-Capodichino - NAP)**
   - **Location:** Situated approximately 4 miles (7 kilometers) northeast of Naples city center, this airport is your primary gateway to both Naples and the Amalfi Coast.

- o Facilities:NAP offers a range of amenities, including dining options, shopping outlets, and car rental services. The airport is well-regarded for its efficiency and friendly staff, ensuring a pleasant arrival experience.
- o Contact Information:
  - Address: Viale Fulco Ruffo di Calabria, 80144 Napoli NA, Italy
  - Website: https://www.aeroportodinapoli.it /en/

2. **Salerno Costa d'Amalfi Airport (Aeroporto di Salerno Costa d'Amalfi - QSR)**
   - o Location: Located in Pontecagnano, approximately 9 miles (15 kilometers) southeast of Salerno, this airport brings you closer to the Amalfi Coast.
   - o Facilities:Following significant upgrades, including a longer runway and new parking areas, Salerno Airport is enhancing its services to accommodate more flights and passengers. A new terminal is expected to open in 2026, further improving the travel experience.
   - o Contact Information:
     - Address: Via Olmo, 84098 Pontecagnano Faiano SA, Italy
     - Website: https://www.aeroportosalerno.it/

Airlines and Flight Options

In 2025, several airlines are expanding their services to Naples and Salerno, making it easier than ever to reach this stunning region.

- **Delta Air Lines**: Starting May 2025, Delta will offer four-times-weekly flights from Atlanta to Naples, complementing its existing New York-JFK to Naples route.
- **American Airlines**:American Airlines is introducing nonstop flights from Chicago O'Hare International Airport (ORD) to Naples, becoming the only airline offering this route.
- **United Airlines**: Continuing its double-daily service from Newark Liberty International Airport (EWR) to Naples, United provides convenient options for travelers from the U.S. East Coast.
- **EasyJet and Ryanair**: Both carriers have commenced flights to Salerno Costa d'Amalfi Airport, offering budget-friendly options from various European cities.

Travel Tips

- **Booking**: Given the increasing popularity of the Amalfi Coast, especially with the new flight options in 2025, it's advisable to book your flights well in advance to secure the best deals.
- **Arrival**: Upon landing at Naples International Airport, you can reach the city center via taxi, bus, or car rental. The Alibus shuttle service connects the airport to key locations in Naples, including the central train station.
- **Proceeding to the Amalfi Coast**: From Naples, you can take a train to Salerno and then a ferry to Amalfi or Positano. Alternatively, private

transfers and car rentals are available for direct travel to your coastal destination.

- **From Salerno Airport**: With its proximity to the Amalfi Coast, Salerno Airport offers convenient access. Car rentals, taxis, and shuttle services can transport you to various coastal towns efficiently.

By Train

Embarking on a journey to Naples and the Amalfi Coast by train in 2025 is both convenient and scenic. Let's explore how you can make the most of this experience.

Reaching Naples by Train

If you're starting from Rome, high-speed trains operated by Trenitalia's Frecciarossa and Italo Treno offer frequent services to Naples. The journey typically takes about 1 hour and 10 minutes, with trains departing from Roma Termini station and arriving at Napoli Centrale. Ticket prices range from €12 to €65, depending on the class and booking time. The first train leaves Rome at 5:31 a.m., and the last departs at 11:58 p.m., providing flexibility for your travel plans.

Napoli Centrale Station

Napoli Centrale is the main train station in Naples, located at Piazza Garibaldi. It's a bustling hub with amenities like restaurants, shops, and car rental services. The station operates daily from early morning until late at night, aligning with train schedules. For assistance, you can visit the information desks or contact the station through their official website.

Traveling from Naples to the Amalfi Coast

While the Amalfi Coast doesn't have direct train services, you can reach it via Salerno or Sorrento.

- **Naples to Salerno**: Regional trains run regularly from Napoli Centrale to Salerno, with an average journey time of 40 minutes. Tickets are affordable, starting from €5.50. Salerno's train station is centrally located, making it easy to transition to other modes of transport. **Website:** Trainline
- **Salerno to Amalfi Coast**: From Salerno, you can take a ferry to various Amalfi Coast towns like Amalfi and Positano. Ferries operate frequently, especially during peak tourist seasons, offering a scenic and enjoyable ride along the coast.

Alternative Route via Sorrento

Another option is to take the Circumvesuviana train from Napoli Garibaldi station (adjacent to Napoli Centrale) to Sorrento. The journey takes about 1 hour and 10 minutes. From Sorrento, buses and ferries are available to different parts of the Amalfi Coast. This route is particularly popular among tourists for its convenience and the beautiful views along the way.

Travel Tips

- **Booking Tickets**: It's advisable to book high-speed train tickets in advance to secure the best prices and availability. For regional trains, tickets can be purchased on the day of travel.
- **Luggage**: Most trains have ample luggage space, but during peak times, storage can be limited. Traveling with manageable luggage will make your journey more comfortable.

- **Schedules**: Train schedules can vary, especially on weekends and holidays. Always check the latest timetables on the official Trenitalia or Italo websites before planning your trip.

B.Transportation Options

Traveling around Naples and the Amalfi Coast in 2025 offers you two exciting options: ferries and cars. Each mode of transport has its own charm and practical advantages, depending on how you want to experience this stunning region. Let's dive into the details so you can make the best choice for your trip.

Ferries

If you want to soak in the jaw-dropping views of the Amalfi Coast while avoiding the hassle of navigating narrow roads, ferries are your best bet. Traveling by water is not just a mode of transport here—it's an unforgettable experience.

- **Where Ferries Operate**:
  Ferries connect key locations along the Amalfi Coast and nearby areas. Major routes include:
    o Naples to Sorrento, Amalfi, and Positano.
    o Salerno to Amalfi, Positano, and Capri.
    o Sorrento to Capri, Amalfi, and Ischia.
- **Major Ferry Operators**:
    o **Alilauro**: Specializing in routes between Naples, Sorrento, and the islands. www.alilauro.it
    o **Travelmar**: Known for excellent service along the Amalfi Coast, with frequent

stops at Positano, Amalfi, and Salerno.www.travelmar.it
  o **NLG (Navigazione Libera del Golfo)**: Operating routes from Naples to Capri and the Amalfi Coast.www.navlib.it
- **Cost and Schedule**: Ferry prices vary depending on the route but generally range from €10 to €30 one-way. During peak season (May to September), ferries operate frequently, with departures every 30–60 minutes. Off-season schedules are more limited, so check in advance.
- **Booking and Boarding**: Tickets can be booked online or purchased at ferry terminals. Arrive at least 20–30 minutes early to ensure a smooth boarding process.
- **Pros of Ferries**:
  o Unparalleled coastal views.
  o Avoid traffic congestion.
  o Convenient for island hopping (Capri, Ischia, Procida).
- **Cons of Ferries**:
  o Weather-dependent—services may be canceled during rough seas.
  o Limited nighttime service.

Cars

For those who prefer to explore at their own pace, renting a car is an excellent option. Having your own vehicle gives you the freedom to visit hidden gems and off-the-beaten-path locations that aren't easily accessible by public transport.

- **Driving Along the Amalfi Coast**: The famous SS163 (Amalfi Drive) is one of the most scenic roads in the world, but it's not for the faint-hearted. The road is narrow and winding, often with hairpin turns and steep drop-offs. Traffic can be heavy in peak season, but the breathtaking views make it worth the challenge.

- **Car Rental Options:**
  Major rental companies like Hertz, Europcar, and Avis have offices at Naples International Airport and in downtown Naples. Smaller local rental companies may offer competitive rates, but always read reviews and check insurance policies carefully.
- **Cost:**
  Car rental prices start at around €40–€60 per day, depending on the car type and season. Fuel and parking fees are additional costs to consider.
- **Parking:**
  Parking can be a headache, especially in small coastal towns like Positano and Amalfi, where spaces are limited and expensive (€3–€5 per hour on average). Public parking lots are your best bet, but they fill up quickly.
- **Tips for Driving:**
  - Opt for a compact car—it's easier to navigate the tight roads.
  - Use GPS or a reliable navigation app to avoid getting lost.
  - Drive cautiously and yield to local buses and delivery vans on narrow roads.

Which Option is Right for You?

- **Choose Ferries If:**
  You prefer a relaxing, hassle-free experience with stunning coastal views. Ferries are ideal for

visiting multiple towns along the coast or exploring islands like Capri.

- **Choose Cars If:**
  You want the freedom to stop wherever you like and explore less-touristy areas. A car is perfect for adventurers who don't mind the challenge of navigating narrow roads.

C.Navigating Local transport

Public Buses

Public buses are one of the most economical ways to travel in Naples and along the Amalfi Coast. While they're not the fastest option, they are reliable and provide a true local experience.

- **In Naples:**
  - Operated by **ANM (Azienda Napoletana Mobilità)**, the city's buses connect major areas like Piazza Garibaldi (near Napoli Centrale station), the historic center, and the Vomero district.
  - Tickets: A single ride costs around €1.20, and you can purchase tickets at tobacco shops (*tabaccherie*), kiosks, or directly via the Unico Campania app.
  - Tip: Validate your ticket when boarding, as inspectors occasionally check.
- **Along the Amalfi Coast:**
  - **SITA Buses** are the primary public transport option for towns like Positano, Amalfi, and Ravello. These buses are affordable (around €2–€6 depending on

the route) but can get very crowded, especially in summer.

- ○ **Best Routes:**
  - ■ Amalfi to Ravello: A quick 20-minute ride through scenic mountain roads.
  - ■ Amalfi to Positano: Approximately 40 minutes of stunning coastal views.
- **Pro Tip:** Arrive early at bus stops during peak hours, as buses fill up quickly and standing room is limited.

Metro and Funiculars in Naples

Naples' metro and funicular systems are excellent for navigating the city's hilly terrain.

- **Metro:**
  - ○ The **Metro Line 1** (known as the "Art Line") is a tourist attraction in itself, featuring beautifully designed stations like Toledo, often hailed as one of the most stunning metro stops in the world.
  - ○ Operating Hours: 6:00 AM to 11:00 PM, with trains every 8–12 minutes.
- **Funiculars:**
  - ○ Naples has four funicular lines connecting the city's lower areas to the hilltop Vomero district. These short rides offer spectacular views and are perfect for avoiding uphill walks.
- **Tickets:** A single metro or funicular ride costs €1.20, with day passes available for around €4.50.

Taxis and Rideshares

Taxis are widely available in Naples but less so along the Amalfi Coast. While they're convenient, especially late at night or when buses aren't running, fares can add up quickly.

- **Taxis in Naples:**
    - Official taxis are white with a "TAXI" sign on top. Always check that the meter is running or agree on a fare in advance.
    - Typical Costs: A short ride within Naples costs €10–€20, while airport transfers are fixed at €20–€25 to the city center.
- **Taxis on the Amalfi Coast:**
    - Expect higher rates, with rides from Amalfi to Positano costing around €50–€80. Pre-arranged transfers can save you some hassle.
- **Rideshares:**
    - Apps like Uber and Free Now are available in Naples but not widely used along the Amalfi Coast. In coastal towns, local taxi services are the go-to.

Navigating Coastal Roads

For a more adventurous and flexible option, consider renting a scooter or e-bike.

- **Scooters:**
    - Ideal for solo travelers or couples. Rates start at €30–€50 per day.
    - Recommended for experienced drivers due to narrow, winding roads.
- **E-Bikes:**

- A fantastic eco-friendly option for exploring villages and short distances. Rentals are available for €20–€40 per day.

Tips for Stress-Free Navigation

1. **Download Travel Apps**: Apps like Moovit, Google Maps, and Unico Campania are invaluable for real-time schedules and route planning.
2. **Be Punctual**: Public transport in Naples is fairly punctual, but Amalfi Coast buses can run behind schedule, especially during summer.
3. **Cash**: While many services accept cards, having small change for tickets and tips is always a good idea.

Chapter 3: When to Visit

A.Seasonal Highlights

Spring (March to May):
Spring is one of the best times to visit Naples and the Amalfi Coast. The weather is mild, with temperatures ranging from 55°F to 75°F (13°C to 24°C), and the region is blanketed in lush greenery and colorful blooms. It's perfect for outdoor activities like hiking the Path of the Gods or strolling through Naples' historic streets. Crowds are thinner compared to summer, and hotel prices are often more reasonable.

Summer (June to August):
Summer is the peak season, drawing tourists from around the globe. Expect sunny days with temperatures between 75°F and 90°F (24°C to 32°C). Coastal towns like Positano and Amalfi buzz with energy, and ferries run frequently, making it easy to explore the coastline. However, crowds are at their highest, and

accommodation prices skyrocket. Book in advance if you plan to visit during this time. Beaches are lively, and the nightlife in Naples is lively and exciting.

Autumn (September to November):
Autumn rivals spring as an ideal time to visit. The summer crowds thin out, but the weather remains warm and pleasant, with temperatures ranging from 60°F to 80°F (15°C to 27°C). This is harvest season, so you'll find local festivals celebrating wine, olives, and chestnuts. The sea is still warm enough for swimming, and hiking trails are less crowded. It's a more peaceful, authentic experience.

Winter (December to February):
Winter is the off-season, but it has its own allure. Naples comes alive with Christmas markets, nativity displays, and traditional holiday treats. Temperatures hover around 50°F to 60°F (10°C to 15°C), making it chilly but manageable. The Amalfi Coast is much quieter, with many hotels and restaurants closing for the season, but you'll have a chance to enjoy the stunning landscapes without the crowds. If you're traveling for culture and history, winter is a great time to visit Naples' museums and ruins.

B.Festivals and Events to Plan Around

Spring Festivals (March-May)

1. **Easter Week (Settimana Santa) – Late March or Early April**
   - **Where:** Naples and coastal towns like Amalfi and Sorrento.

- o **Why Go**: Easter in southern Italy is a deeply spiritual and vibrant celebration. Witness solemn processions, elaborate religious ceremonies, and colorful parades. In Naples, the Via Crucis procession winds through the city's historic streets, while Amalfi hosts beautiful coastal processions with candles illuminating the night.
- o **Insider Tip**: Try *pastiera napoletana*, a sweet ricotta and orange blossom tart traditionally eaten during Easter.

2. **Sagra della Zeppola – March 19th**
   - o **Where**:Naples(all through Campania).
   - o **Why Go**:Celebrate St. Joseph's Day with *zeppole*, a traditional cream-filled pastry topped with powdered sugar and cherries. Bakeries and street vendors offer freshly made delights all day.
   - o **Insider Tip**: Head to local bakeries early to snag the freshest *zeppole*.

Summer Festivals (June-August)

1. **Festa di Sant'Andrea – June 27th and November 30th**
   - o **Where**: Amalfi.
   - o **Why Go**:This festival honors Amalfi's patron saint with a day full of processions, music, and fireworks. In June, the summer event is particularly lively, with the entire town gathering to celebrate.
   - o **Insider Tip**: Watch the procession carry the statue of Saint Andrew down to the waterfront—an awe-inspiring tradition.

2. **Ravello Festival – July to September**
   o **Where**: Ravello.
   o **Why Go**: This internationally renowned arts festival takes place in the gardens of Villa Rufolo, offering performances of music, dance, and theater. The views from the venue are as stunning as the art itself.
   o **Insider Tip**: Book tickets in advance, as this festival is hugely popular with both locals and visitors.
3. **Positano Opera Festival – July and August**
   o **Where**: Positano.
   o **Why Go**: Experience opera in an intimate seaside setting. Performances are held in small, scenic venues, creating an unforgettable cultural experience.

Autumn Festivals (September-November)

1. **Grape Harvest Festivals – September and October**
   o **Where**:Various villages across Campania, including Ravello and Furore.
   o **Why Go**:Celebrate the grape harvest with wine tastings, food stalls, and local music. These festivals showcase the region's winemaking heritage and offer a chance to sample some of the best local vintages.
   o **Insider Tip**: Look for events hosted by smaller, family-run wineries for a more authentic experience.

2. **Chestnut Festival (Sagra della Castagna) – October**
   - ○ **Where:** Scala (near Ravello).
   - ○ **Why Go:**This cozy festival celebrates the humble chestnut with roasted chestnuts, chestnut desserts, and savory dishes. It's a delightful way to experience autumn in the mountains.

Winter Festivals (December-February)

1. **Naples Christmas Markets – December**
   - ○ **Where:**Via San Gregorio Armeno, Naples.
   - ○ **Why Go:**This street transforms into a festive wonderland, featuring handcrafted nativity figurines, holiday decorations, and local treats. Naples is famous for its elaborate nativity scenes (*presepi*), and this market is the best place to see (and buy) them.
   - ○ **Insider Tip:** Don't miss the live nativity displays at local churches—they're works of art in themselves.
2. **New Year's Eve in Naples – December 31st**
   - ○ **Where:**Naples waterfront and Piazza del Plebiscito.
   - ○ **Why Go:**Naples throws a grand party to welcome the New Year, complete with fireworks over the Bay of Naples, live music, and dancing in the streets.
   - ○ **Insider Tip:**Head to the Lungomare Caracciolo promenade for the best views of the fireworks.
3. **Festival of Lights (Festa della Luminaria) – February**

- **Where**: Minori.
- **Why Go**:This lesser-known festival features candlelit processions and illuminates the town in honor of its patron saint. It's a peaceful and reflective event in the quieter winter months.

Chapter 4: Exploring Naples

A. Top Attractions in Naples

1. Naples National Archaeological Museum (Museo Archeologico Nazionale di Napoli)

Description and History: This museum houses one of the most extensive collections of Greco-Roman artifacts in the world, including treasures from Pompeii and Herculaneum. The intricate mosaics and sculptures offer a vivid glimpse into ancient life.

Location: Piazza Museo, 19, 80135 Napoli NA, Italy.

How to Get There: Take Metro Line 1 to the Museo station; the museum is a short walk away.

What to Do There: Explore exhibits featuring ancient art, artifacts, and the renowned Farnese Collection.

Where to Stay Nearby: Consider accommodations in the historic center for easy access.

What to Eat and Drink: Nearby, enjoy authentic Neapolitan pizza at local pizzerias.

Cost: Admission is approximately €18.

Best Time to Visit: Weekday mornings to avoid crowds.

How to Book: Tickets can be purchased on-site or online.

Website: Museo Archeologico Nazionale di Napoli

Opening Hours: Wednesday to Monday, 9:00 AM to 7:30 PM.

2. Castel dell'Ovo

Description and History: As Naples' oldest standing fortification, this "Egg Castle" offers panoramic views of the Gulf of Naples. Its name stems from a legend about a magical egg hidden within its foundations.

Location: Via Eldorado, 3, 80132 Napoli NA, Italy.

How to Get There: A pleasant walk along the seafront from the city center.

What to Do There: Explore the castle's terraces and courtyards, and enjoy art exhibitions often held inside.

Where to Stay Nearby: Seafront hotels offer stunning views.

What to Eat and Drink: Savor seafood at nearby restaurants in Borgo Marinari.

Cost: Entry is free.

Best Time to Visit: Late afternoon for sunset views.

How to Book: No booking required.

<u>Website:</u> Castel dell'Ovo

<u>Opening Hours:</u> Monday to Saturday, 9:00 AM to 7:30 PM; Sundays and holidays, 9:00 AM to 2:00 PM.

3. Spaccanapoli

<u>Description and History:</u> This narrow street cuts through Naples' historic center, embodying the city's vibrant spirit with its shops, churches, and bustling atmosphere.

<u>Location:</u> Historic center of Naples.

<u>How to Get There:</u> Accessible by foot from most central locations.

<u>What to Do There:</u> Visit artisan workshops, taste local street food, and admire historical buildings.

<u>Where to Stay Nearby:</u> Boutique hotels in the historic center immerse you in local life.

<u>What to Eat and Drink:</u> Try sfogliatelle pastries and espresso from local cafés.

Cost: Free to explore.

Best Time to Visit: Evenings, when the street comes alive.

How to Book: No booking necessary.

4. Pompeii Archaeological Site

Description and History: The ancient city of Pompeii, buried by Mount Vesuvius in 79 AD, offers a remarkable snapshot of Roman life frozen in time.

Location: Pompei, Metropolitan City of Naples, Italy.

How to Get There: Take the Circumvesuviana train from Naples to Pompei Scavi-Villa dei Misteri station.

What to Do There: Explore well-preserved ruins, including homes, temples, and theaters.

Where to Stay Nearby: Accommodations in Naples or Sorrento are convenient.

What to Eat and Drink: Cafés near the entrance offer refreshments.

Cost: Admission is approximately €16.

Best Time to Visit: Early morning to avoid heat and crowds.

How to Book: Purchase tickets online or at the entrance.

Website: Pompeii Archaeological Site

Opening Hours: Daily, 9:00 AM to 7:00 PM.

5. Naples Underground (Napoli Sotterranea)

Description and History: Beneath Naples lies a labyrinth of tunnels and caves dating back to ancient

Greek and Roman times, used over centuries for various purposes.

Location: Piazza San Gaetano, 68, 80138 Napoli NA, Italy.

How to Get There: Located in the historic center; a short walk from major attractions.

What to Do There: Take guided tours to explore ancient cisterns, WWII shelters, and underground theaters.

Where to Stay Nearby: Stay in the historic center for a seamless experience. Many boutique hotels and B&Bs in the area offer charming stays within walking distance.

What to Eat and Drink: After your tour, indulge in a hearty Neapolitan meal at a nearby trattoria. Try a classic pasta alla genovese or parmigiana di melanzane to refuel.

Cost: Guided tours typically cost around €10–€15 per person, depending on the type of experience and duration.

Best Time to Visit: Late afternoon or early evening for a cooler and quieter tour.

How to Book: You can book tickets online through official tour providers or on-site at the entrance. Advance booking is recommended, especially in peak travel months.

Website: Visit Napoli Sotterranea for updated schedules, tour options, and booking.

Opening Hours: Guided tours are available daily, with start times typically ranging from 10:00 AM to 7:00 PM.

B. Hidden Gems and Local Experiences

1. Rione Sanità District

Why It's Special:
Once overlooked, Rione Sanità has undergone a cultural renaissance and is now a vibrant neighborhood filled with history, street art, and authentic local life. It's home to historic palaces, colorful murals, and one of Naples' most fascinating ossuaries.

What to Do:

- Visit the **Fontanelle Cemetery**, an eerie but captivating ossuary where thousands of human skulls are neatly arranged—a haunting reminder of Naples' past.

- Explore **Palazzo Sanfelice** and **Palazzo dello Spagnolo**, two stunning examples of Neapolitan baroque architecture with unique staircases.
- Stroll through lively streets lined with vendors selling fresh produce, pastries, and flowers.

Where to Eat:
Stop at **Concettina ai Tre Santi**, a beloved pizzeria known for its innovative takes on traditional Neapolitan pizza.

How to Get There:
Take Metro Line 1 to the Materdei station, then walk a short distance into the district.

2. Parco Vergiliano a Piedigrotta

Why It's Special:
This peaceful park, often confused with the larger Parco Virgiliano, is tucked away in the Piedigrotta area. It's a serene spot where the tombs of the poet Virgil and the philosopher Giacomo Leopardi are said to rest.

What to Do:

- Reflect on the city's literary history while surrounded by greenery and quiet pathways.
- Enjoy views of the Gulf of Naples from this hidden oasis.

Where to Eat:
Nearby cafes along the Mergellina promenade serve fresh pastries and espresso, perfect for a quick break.

How to Get There:
Take Metro Line 2 to Mergellina station, then follow signs to the park.

3. Galleria Borbonica (Bourbon Tunnel)

Why It's Special:
This underground network of tunnels and chambers was originally constructed in the 19th century as an escape route for King Ferdinand II. It later served as a shelter during World War II.

What to Do:

- Take a guided tour through the tunnels to see historic artifacts, vintage vehicles, and graffiti left by WWII evacuees.
- Marvel at engineering and learn about Naples' complex history beneath its bustling streets.

How to Book:
Tickets are available online at the Galleria Borbonica website or at the entrance. Guided tours cost around €10–€15.

How to Get There:
The entrance is near Piazza Plebiscito, easily accessible by foot or taxi.

4. Borgo Marinari

Why It's Special:
This charming fishing village, located on the islet of Megaride, feels like stepping back in time. It's a quiet escape from the city's hustle and bustle.

What to Do:

- Walk along the marina and admire the small fishing boats bobbing in the water.

- Visit **Castel dell'Ovo**, which looms nearby, offering stunning views of the coastline.
- Enjoy a leisurely seafood dinner at one of the waterfront restaurants.

Where to Eat:
Try **Ristorante La Scialuppa** for fresh fish and unbeatable views.

How to Get There:
It's a short walk from Naples' city center, near the Lungomare promenade.

5. Naples Metro Art Stations

Why It's Special:
The Naples Metro is more than just public transportation—it's a world-class art gallery. Several stations, like **Toledo**, **Università**, and **Dante**, feature contemporary art installations and architectural masterpieces.

What to Do:

- Spend time admiring the vibrant mosaics, sculptures, and light displays.
- Take photos of the famous Toledo Station, often considered one of the most beautiful metro stations in the world.

Cost:
A single metro ticket costs €1.20, making this one of the most affordable ways to enjoy art in the city.

How to Get There:
Simply hop on Metro Line 1 and explore station by station.

6. Porta Nolana Market

Why It's Special:
This bustling street market is the perfect place to experience the energy of Naples. It's known for its fresh seafood, seasonal produce, and local specialties.

What to Do:

- Shop for local ingredients like sun-dried tomatoes, mozzarella, and citrus fruits.
- Interact with friendly vendors and immerse yourself in the vibrant atmosphere.

What to Eat:
Try freshly fried seafood or pick up some street food like *arancini* (stuffed rice balls) or *zeppole* (fried dough).

How to Get There:
The market is near Napoli Centrale station, a short walk from the Piazza Garibaldi area.

Pro Tips for Discovering Hidden Gems

1. **Ask Locals for Recommendations:**
   Neapolitans are proud of their city and often happy to share their favorite hidden spots.
2. **Explore Beyond the Tourist Areas:**
   Wander off the beaten path to find authentic neighborhoods and experiences.
3. **Embrace the Unexpected:**
   Some of the best moments in Naples happen when you stumble upon something unplanned, like a lively piazza or a quiet courtyard.

C.Nightlife

1. Piazza Bellini:

Why It's Special:
Piazza Bellini is where students, locals, and tourists mingle in an effortlessly cool atmosphere. Surrounded by ancient ruins and historic buildings, this square buzzes with life after sunset.

What to Do:

- Grab an *aperitivo* (pre-dinner drink) at one of the many outdoor bars and cafés.
- Enjoy live music performances, which often pop up spontaneously.
- People-watch as locals gather to chat, laugh, and toast to the night.

Where to Go:

- **Caffè Arabo:** Known for its relaxed vibe and affordable drinks.
- **Spazio Nea:** A stylish café and gallery that turns into a lively bar in the evenings.

Best Time to Visit:
From 7:00 PM onwards, as the square fills with energy and activity.

2. Chiaia District

Why It's Special:
If you're looking for a more upscale evening, head to Chiaia, Naples' chic and trendy neighborhood. This area is home to elegant wine bars, sophisticated cocktail lounges, and exclusive clubs.

What to Do:

- Enjoy expertly crafted cocktails at stylish bars.
- Explore intimate wine lounges that showcase Campania's finest vintages.
- Dance the night away at exclusive clubs frequented by Naples' fashionable crowd.

Where to Go:

- **Barril:** A classy bar known for its creative cocktails and live DJ sets.
- **Cantine Sociali:** A cozy wine bar offering a curated selection of local and international wines.
- **Bluestone:** A jazz club with incredible live performances in an intimate setting.

Best Time to Visit:
Start your evening with drinks around 8:00 PM, and head to clubs after midnight.

3. Lungomare Caracciolo

Why It's Special:
Naples' waterfront promenade transforms into a magical spot at night, offering breathtaking views of the Bay of Naples and Mount Vesuvius under the stars.

What to Do:

- Stroll along the promenade and enjoy the sea breeze.
- Dine al fresco at one of the many seaside restaurants.
- End your night at a bar with a terrace overlooking the water.

Where to Go:

- **Ristorante La Bersagliera:** Perfect for a romantic dinner with views of Castel dell'Ovo.
- **Officina 31:** A trendy bar offering creative cocktails and light bites.

Best Time to Visit:
After 9:00 PM, when the lights of the city reflect beautifully on the water.

4. Underground Bars and Hidden Gems

Why It's Special:
Naples has a growing number of speakeasies and underground bars that offer a unique and intimate nightlife experience.

What to Do:

- Discover hidden bars tucked away in the city's alleys.

- Enjoy signature cocktails and live music in a cozy, eclectic atmosphere.

Where to Go:

- **L'Antiquario:** A renowned speakeasy-style bar with expertly crafted drinks.
- **Archivio Storico:** A stylish cocktail bar with a historical theme, serving drinks inspired by Naples' past.

Best Time to Visit:
From 10:00 PM onwards, as these spots get busier later in the evening.

5. Nightclubs and Late-Night Venues

Why It's Special:
For those who want to keep the party going, Naples has a selection of lively nightclubs where you can dance until dawn.

What to Do:

- Experience electronic music, live DJs, and themed parties.
- Meet locals and fellow travelers on the dance floor.

Where to Go:

- **Arenile di Bagnoli:** A beachfront club hosting open-air parties with a mix of live music and DJs.
- **Duel Beat:** A favorite for electronic music enthusiasts, offering multiple dance floors and a vibrant atmosphere.

Best Time to Visit:
Clubs usually get going after midnight and stay open until 4:00 AM or later.

6. Local Traditions

Why It's Special:
In Naples, nightlife doesn't always mean loud music and dancing. Locals often end their evenings with a quiet coffee or a sweet treat at a late-night café.

What to Do:

- Sip on a *caffè corretto* (espresso with a splash of liquor) or a creamy *caffè nocciola* (hazelnut coffee).
- Indulge in a warm *sfogliatella* e babà *al rum*.

Where to Go:

- **Gambrinus:** A historic café near Piazza del Plebiscito, perfect for a late-night espresso.
- **Scaturchio:** A beloved pasticceria known for its decadent desserts.

Best Time to Visit:
After 10:00 PM, when the cafés have a relaxed, intimate atmosphere.

Tips for Enjoying Naples' Nightlife

1. **Dress Smart:**
   While casual attire is fine in many places, some upscale bars and clubs have a dress code.
2. **Plan Your Transport:**
   Public transport options like the metro stop running around 11:00 PM, so arrange a taxi or

use ridesharing apps to get back to your accommodation.

3. **Embrace the Atmosphere:**
    Naples' nightlife is as much about connection and community as it is about entertainment. Don't be shy—join in conversations and make new friends.

Chapter 5: Exploring Amalfi Coast

A.Must Visit Villages

1. Positano

Description and History: Positano is renowned for its colorful, cliffside houses that cascade down to the Mediterranean Sea. Historically a fishing village, it transformed into a glamorous destination attracting artists and celebrities.

Location: Situated on the western part of the Amalfi Coast, Positano is approximately 60 kilometers from Naples.

How to Reach: You can reach Positano by ferry from Naples or Sorrento, or by bus along the coastal road.

What to Do:

- **Explore:** Wander through narrow streets lined with boutiques and art galleries.
- **Relax:** Unwind on Spiaggia Grande, the main beach, or take a boat trip to nearby coves.
- **Visit:** Admire the Church of Santa Maria Assunta, known for its majolica-tiled dome.

Where to Stay: Consider staying at Hotel Poseidon for its stunning views and excellent service.

What to Eat and Drink: Savor fresh seafood at Chez Black, a renowned beachfront restaurant.

Best Time to Visit: Late spring to early autumn offers pleasant weather and a vibrant atmosphere.

2. Amalfi

Description and History: Once a powerful maritime republic, Amalfi boasts a rich history evident in its architecture and culture.

Location: Centrally located on the Amalfi Coast, it's about 75 kilometers from Naples.

How to Reach: Accessible by ferry, bus, or car from Naples and Salerno.

What to Do:

- **Visit:** Explore the Amalfi Cathedral, an architectural marvel with a blend of styles.
- **Learn:** Discover the Paper Museum to understand Amalfi's papermaking heritage.
- **Stroll:** Enjoy the lively Piazza del Duomo, filled with cafes and shops.

Where to Stay: Hotel Marina Riviera offers comfortable accommodations with panoramic views.

What to Eat and Drink: Try the local specialty, Scialatielli ai Frutti di Mare, at Trattoria da Gemma.

Best Time to Visit: May to September, when festivals and events enliven the town.

3. Ravello

Description and History: Perched high above the coast, Ravello is known for its tranquil ambiance and artistic heritage.

Location: Located 365 meters above sea level, it's about 5 kilometers from Amalfi.

How to Reach: Reachable by bus or car from Amalfi; the winding roads offer scenic views.

What to Do:

- **Visit:** Explore Villa Rufolo and Villa Cimbrone, famed for their gardens and vistas.

- **Experience:** Attend the Ravello Festival, featuring music and cultural events.
- **Relax:** Enjoy a peaceful walk through the town's charming streets.

Where to Stay: Belmond Hotel Caruso provides luxury accommodations with historical charm.

What to Eat and Drink: Dine at Rossellinis for gourmet Italian cuisine with a view.

Best Time to Visit: Summer months, especially during the festival season.

4. Atrani

Description and History: As one of Italy's smallest towns, Atrani retains its authentic charm with medieval structures and a serene beach.

Location: Adjacent to Amalfi, it's just a short walk away.

How to Reach: Easily accessible on foot from Amalfi or by local bus.

What to Do:

- **Explore:** Wander through the labyrinth of alleys and arches.
- **Relax:** Spend time on the quiet, sandy beach.
- **Visit:** See the Church of San Salvatore de' Birecto, dating back to the 10th century.

Where to Stay: Palazzo Ferraioli offers modern amenities in a historic setting.

What to Eat and Drink: Enjoy local dishes at A Paranza, known for its seafood.

Best Time to Visit: Spring and autumn, to avoid crowds and enjoy mild weather.

5. Praiano

Description and History: Once a fishing village, Praiano is now a tranquil retreat known for its sunsets and artisan shops.

Location: Between Positano and Amalfi, it's about 10 kilometers from each.

How to Reach: Accessible by SITA bus or car along the coastal road.

What to Do:

- **Visit:** See the Church of San Gennaro, with its beautiful tiled floor.
- **Relax:** Enjoy Marina di Praia, a secluded beach.
- **Explore:** Discover local art galleries and ceramic shops.

Where to Stay: Hotel Margherita offers comfortable rooms with sea views.

What to Eat and Drink: Dine at Il Pirata, set on a cliffside with panoramic views.

Best Time to Visit: Late spring to early autumn for beach activities and festivals.

Tips for Visiting:

- **Booking Accommodations:** It's advisable to book hotels in advance, especially during peak season.
- **Use Public Transport:** Ferries and SITA buses are the most convenient ways to explore the Amalfi Coast. They're affordable, scenic, and save you the stress of driving on narrow, winding roads.
- **Wear Comfortable Shoes:** Many of these villages have steep streets and stairs, so sturdy footwear is essential.

- **Arrive Early:** For the best experience, start your day early to avoid crowds, especially in popular spots like Positano and Amalfi.
- **Pack Light:** If you plan to stay overnight or explore multiple villages, keep your luggage light for easy mobility.

How to Book and Plan Your Visits

- **Accommodations:** Use platforms like Booking.com or Airbnb to reserve your stay well in advance. For luxury hotels, book directly through their official websites for the best deals and perks.
- **Tours and Activities:** Consider guided tours to enhance your experience. Websites like GetYourGuide and Viator offer curated packages for activities like hiking, boat trips, and wine tastings.
- **Transportation:** Check ferry schedules on Travelmar or Alilauro to plan your journeys between villages. For buses, purchase tickets at local tabaccherie (tobacco shops).

B.Outdoor Adventures

1. Hike the Path of the Gods (Sentiero degli Dei)

Why It's Special:
Known as one of the most beautiful trails in the world, the Path of the Gods offers sweeping views of the coastline, terraced vineyards, and charming villages perched on the cliffs.

Route:

- The trail begins in Bomerano (Agerola) and ends in Nocelle, a hamlet above Positano.
- Distance: Approximately 7.8 kilometers (4.8 miles).
- Duration: 2.5–3 hours of moderate hiking.

What to Expect:

- Beautiful views of the Mediterranean and Capri in the distance.
- Ancient mule paths, stone steps, and picturesque rural landscapes.

Tips:

- Wear sturdy hiking shoes, as some parts of the trail are rocky and uneven.
- Start early to avoid the midday heat and crowds.
- Bring water, snacks, and a camera to capture the stunning scenery.

Cost:
Free to hike. Guided tours cost around €40–€60 per person.

How to Get There:
Take a bus or taxi to Bomerano from Amalfi or Positano. Return via local bus from Nocelle or continue walking to Positano.

2. Kayaking and Paddleboarding

Why It's Special:
Gliding along the crystal-clear waters of the Amalfi Coast offers a unique perspective of its rugged cliffs, sea caves, and hidden beaches.

Top Spots:

- **Amalfi:** Rent a kayak or paddleboard and explore nearby coves and the famous Grotta dello Smeraldo (Emerald Grotto).
- **Positano:** Paddle along the coastline for stunning views of the colorful village from the water.

Tips:

- Choose early morning or late afternoon for calmer waters and fewer crowds.
- Look for guided tours that include stops at lesser-known beaches and caves.

Cost:
Rentals start at €15–€25 per hour. Guided tours cost around €50–€80 per person.

How to Book:
Check with local water sports companies like Amalfi Kayak Tours.

3. Explore Fiordo di Furore

Why It's Special:
This natural fjord is a dramatic inlet with steep cliffs, a small beach, and an arched bridge often featured in iconic Amalfi Coast photos.

What to Do:

- Swim in the calm waters of the fjord.
- Relax on the tiny beach, surrounded by towering cliffs.

- Hike the nearby trails for panoramic views of the fjord.

Cost:
Free to visit. Parking nearby costs around €5 per hour.

How to Get There:
Accessible by car or SITA bus. There are steps leading down to the beach from the main road.

4. Boat Tours and Snorkeling

Why It's Special:
A boat tour lets you experience the Amalfi Coast's beauty from the sea, and snorkeling allows you to explore its underwater wonders.

Top Experiences:

- **Private Boat Tours:** Ideal for a personalized experience, visiting secluded beaches and iconic sites like the Faraglioni Rocks near Capri.
- **Group Excursions:** Affordable and social, often including snorkeling stops and light refreshments.

Snorkeling Hotspots:

- **Grotta dello Smeraldo:** Famous for its emerald-green waters.
- **Marina di Praia:** A quiet cove perfect for underwater exploration.

Cost:

- Private tours: €300–€600 per boat, depending on duration and group size.

- Group tours: €50–€100 per person.

How to Book:
Use platforms like GetYourGuide or book directly with local operators in Amalfi or Positano.

5. Cycling Along the Amalfi Coast

Why It's Special:
Cycling offers a thrilling way to explore the coastal road while enjoying breathtaking views and fresh sea air.

Best Routes:

- Amalfi to Ravello: A challenging uphill ride with rewarding views.
- Positano to Praiano: A shorter, scenic route along the coastline.

Tips:

- Rent an e-bike if you prefer a more relaxed ride on steep terrain.
- Start early in the day to avoid heavy traffic.

Cost:
Bike rentals start at €20 per day for standard bikes and €40 per day for e-bikes.

How to Book:
Rent bikes from local shops like Agerola Bike or ask your hotel for recommendations.

6. Cliff Jumping and Swimming in Hidden Coves

Why It's Special:
The Amalfi Coast's rugged coastline is dotted with

hidden coves and natural swimming pools, perfect for thrill-seekers and beach lovers.

Top Spots:

- **Nerano:** A small fishing village with nearby coves ideal for swimming and snorkeling.
- **Conca dei Marini:** Known for its crystal-clear waters and peaceful atmosphere.

Tips:

- Always check water depth and conditions before jumping.
- Pack water shoes to navigate rocky areas.

Cost:
Most coves are free to access. Some private beaches may charge an entry fee of €10–€20.

7. Sunset Views from Mount Tre Calli

Why It's Special:
For a less crowded hiking experience, head to Mount Tre Calli near Bomerano. The trail offers incredible sunset views over the Amalfi Coast.

Trail Details:

- Distance: 7 kilometers (4.3 miles) round trip.
- Duration: 3 hours.

Tips:

- Bring a flashlight if you plan to return after sunset.
- Pack a picnic to enjoy at the summit.

Cost:
Free to hike.

How to Get There:
Take a bus or taxi to Bomerano and follow the trail signs.

C. Unique Local Cuisine and Dining

The Amalfi Coast isn't just a feast for the eyes—it's a paradise for your taste buds too. Dining here is more than just eating; it's an experience that connects you to the heart and soul of the coast. Let's explore the unique flavors and dining experiences you can savor on your visit.

1. Lemons

Why It's Special:
The Amalfi Coast's iconic lemons, known as *sfusato amalfitano*, are massive, fragrant, and sweeter than typical lemons. They're a cornerstone of local dishes and drinks.

Must-Try Lemon Delights:

- **Limoncello:** A sweet lemon liqueur served as a digestif after meals.
- **Delizia al Limone:** A decadent lemon sponge cake with a tangy cream filling.
- **Granita al Limone:** A refreshing lemon slush, perfect on a hot day.

Where to Try:

- **Pasticceria Sal De Riso (Minori):** Renowned for its lemon desserts.
- **Limoncello Factory Tours (Amalfi):** Visit a local producer to see how this famous liqueur is made.

2. Fresh Seafood

Why It's Special:
The Amalfi Coast's proximity to the Mediterranean means seafood is always fresh and abundant. Fishermen bring in the day's catch, and local chefs transform it into culinary masterpieces.

Must-Try Dishes:

- **Spaghetti alle Vongole:** Spaghetti with clams in a light garlic and white wine sauce.
- **Risotto ai Frutti di Mare:** Creamy risotto loaded with mussels, clams, and prawns.
- **Frittura di Mare:** Lightly fried mixed seafood, including squid and anchovies.

Where to Dine:

- **Trattoria da Gemma (Amalfi):** Famous for its seafood risotto and authentic coastal flavors.
- **Chez Black (Positano):** A beachfront restaurant with a vibrant atmosphere and top-notch seafood dishes.

3. Handmade Pasta

Why It's Special:
The Amalfi Coast is home to unique pasta shapes, like *scialatielli*, a short, thick noodle invented in Amalfi.

These pastas are often paired with fresh seafood or simple, flavorful sauces.

Must-Try Dishes:

- **Scialatielli ai Frutti di Mare:** Scialatielli with a mix of clams, mussels, and prawns.
- **Pasta alla Genovese:** A slow-cooked onion and beef sauce served with pasta.

Where to Eat:

- **Ristorante La Tagliata (Positano):** A family-run restaurant serving homemade pasta with breathtaking views.
- **Lo Smeraldino (Amalfi):** Known for its scialatielli dishes and fresh seafood pairings.

4. Buffalo Mozzarella and Caprese Salad

Why It's Special:
Buffalo mozzarella is a specialty of the Campania region, and it's at its freshest on the Amalfi Coast. Paired with ripe tomatoes and fragrant basil, it creates the iconic *Insalata Caprese*.

Where to Try:

- **Agerola Farms (Agerola):** Visit a local farm to taste mozzarella straight from the source.
- **Il Tridente (Praiano):** A rooftop restaurant serving fresh Caprese salad with a view.

5. Sweet Treats: A Dessert Lover's Dream

Why It's Special:
The Amalfi Coast's desserts are a testament to its rich

culinary heritage, blending local ingredients with indulgent flavors.

Must-Try Sweets:

- **Sfogliatella:** A flaky pastry filled with ricotta and citrus zest.
- **Torta Caprese:** A rich chocolate and almond cake.
- **Cannoli:** Crispy pastry tubes filled with sweet ricotta cream.

Where to Indulge:

- **Andrea Pansa (Amalfi):** A historic pastry shop near the cathedral, perfect for an afternoon treat.
- **Pasticceria La Zagara (Positano):** Known for its creative desserts and coffee.

6. Wine and Local Drinks

Why It's Special:
The Campania region produces exceptional wines, with many vineyards located on the Amalfi Coast's steep terraces. Pairing these wines with local dishes is a highlight of dining here.

Must-Try Wines:

- **Falanghina:** A crisp white wine with citrus notes.
- **Aglianico:** A robust red wine with hints of cherry and spice.
- **Costa d'Amalfi DOC:** Wines produced specifically in this region, known for their unique terroir.

Where to Sip:

- **Marisa Cuomo Winery (Furore):** Tour this famous cliffside vineyard and enjoy a tasting with a view.
- **Local Enotecas:** Small wine shops and bars throughout the coast offer tastings of regional wines.

7. Dining with a View

Why It's Special:
Dining on the Amalfi Coast isn't just about the food—it's about the experience. Many restaurants are perched on cliffs or nestled by the sea, offering unforgettable views to accompany your meal.

Top Scenic Spots:

- **Il Pirata (Praiano):** Dine on fresh seafood while waves crash against the rocks below.
- **Ristorante Torre Normanna (Maiori):** Set in a historic Norman tower, this restaurant offers views and gourmet cuisine.

Chapter 6: Accommodations

A.Best Places to Stay in Naples

1. Luxury Hotels

For travelers seeking elegance, top-notch amenities, and exceptional service, Naples' luxury hotels deliver in style.

- **Grand Hotel Vesuvio**
  - **Why Stay Here:** Situated along the Lungomare waterfront, this historic 5-star hotel offers breathtaking views of the Bay of Naples, Mount Vesuvius, and Capri. The rooftop restaurant is a perfect spot for a romantic dinner.
  - **Location:** Via Partenope 45, Naples.
  - **Cost:** From €450 per night.
  - **Facilities:** Rooftop pool, fine dining, spa, and fitness center.
  - **Website:** Grand Hotel Vesuvio

- **Romeo Hotel**
    - **Why Stay Here:**A modern luxury property with chic design, panoramic views, and a Michelin-starred restaurant. The infinity pool overlooking the harbor is a standout feature.
    - **Location:**Via Cristoforo Colombo 45, Naples.
    - **Cost:** From €500 per night.
    - **Facilities:**Spa, rooftop pool, art collections, and wine bar.
    - **Website:** Romeo Hotel

2. Boutique and Mid-Range Hotels

For a mix of charm, comfort, and affordability, these boutique and mid-range options are excellent choices.

- **Palazzo Caracciolo Napoli - MGallery**
    - **Why Stay Here:** A 16th-century palace turned boutique hotel that blends historic charm with contemporary comfort. Ideal for travelers who want a taste of Naples' history with modern amenities.
    - **Location:** Via Carbonara 112, Naples.
    - **Cost:** From €150 per night.
    - **Facilities:** Courtyard dining, spacious rooms, and a prime location near the historic center.
    - **Website:** Palazzo Caracciolo
- **Hotel Piazza Bellini**
    - **Why Stay Here:** Set in the heart of Naples' historic district, this stylish hotel is perfect for travelers who want easy access to major attractions like

Spaccanapoli and the National Archaeological Museum.

- o **Location:**Via Santa Maria di Costantinopoli 101, Naples.
- o **Cost:** From €120 per night.
- o **Facilities:** Chic rooms, garden terrace, and complimentary breakfast.
- o **Website:** Hotel Piazza Bellini

3. Budget-Friendly Options

Naples offers plenty of affordable accommodations that don't skimp on charm or comfort, perfect for travelers on a budget.

- **Naples Experience Hostel**
  - o **Why Stay Here:** This lively hostel is perfect for backpackers and solo travelers. It offers both dorms and private rooms, as well as organized social activities.
  - o **Location:** Via Filippo Maria Briganti 67, Naples.
  - o **Cost:** From €30 per night for dorms, €70 for private rooms.
  - o **Facilities:**Free breakfast, communal kitchen, and a garden.
  - o **Website:** Naples Experience Hostel
- **B&B Napoli Centrale**
  - o **Why Stay Here:**Located near Napoli Centrale station, this budget-friendly B&B is ideal for travelers on the move. Rooms are cozy, clean, and convenient for exploring the city.
  - o **Location:** Piazza Garibaldi 26, Naples.
  - o **Cost:** From €60 per night.

4. Unique Stays in Naples

For something a little different, Naples offers unique accommodations that add a special touch to your stay.

- **Carten Boutique Hotel**
  - ○ **Why Stay Here:**A boutique hotel with quirky decor, personalized service, and fantastic city views.
  - ○ **Location:** Piazza Bovio 22, Naples.
  - ○ **Cost:** From €140 per night.
- **Hotel San Francesco al Monte**
  - ○ **Why Stay Here:** A converted 16th-century monastery offering panoramic views of Naples and luxurious amenities. The rooftop garden and pool are standout features.
  - ○ **Location:** Corso Vittorio Emanuele 328, Naples.
  - ○ **Cost:** From €180 per night.

Tips for Choosing Accommodations in Naples

1. **Location:**
   - ○ Stay in the historic center for easy access to landmarks like Spaccanapoli and the Archaeological Museum.
   - ○ Choose the Lungomare area for waterfront views and a quieter vibe.
   - ○ Near Napoli Centrale is ideal for quick train connections to Pompeii, Amalfi, and beyond.
2. **Book Early:**
   Naples is a year-round destination, and popular hotels fill up quickly, especially during peak travel seasons.

3. **Ask About Extras:**
   Check if breakfast, parking, or airport transfers are included to maximize your value.
4. **Look for Deals:**
   Platforms like Booking.com or Airbnb often have discounts, especially for longer stays or last-minute bookings.

B. Hotels, Villas, and B&Bs Along the Amalfi Coast

1. Luxury Hotels

If you're seeking unparalleled views and top-tier service, the Amalfi Coast's luxury hotels won't disappoint.

- **Le Sirenuse (Positano)**
  - **Why Stay Here:** This iconic 5-star hotel in the heart of Positano offers stunning views, impeccable service, and an infinity pool overlooking the Mediterranean.
  - **Location:** Via Cristoforo Colombo 30, Positano.
  - **Cost:** From €1,000 per night.
  - **Facilities:** Michelin-starred restaurant, spa, and private boat tours.
  - **Website:** Le Sirenuse
- **Belmond Hotel Caruso (Ravello)**
  - **Why Stay Here:** A former 11th-century palace turned into a luxurious retreat with a legendary infinity pool. It's perfect for couples and honeymooners.
  - **Location:** Piazza San Giovanni del Toro 2, Ravello.

- Cost: From €950 per night.
- Facilities: Fine dining, wellness center, and shuttle service to Amalfi.
- Website: Belmond Hotel Caruso
- **Santa Caterina (Amalfi)**
  - **Why Stay Here:** This elegant hotel offers a private beach club, a clifftop restaurant, and impeccable Italian hospitality.
  - Location: SS Amalfitana 9, Amalfi.
  - Cost: From €850 per night.
  - Facilities: Pool, spa, and free boat transfers.
  - Website: Santa Caterina

2. Charming Villas

For a more intimate and exclusive experience, consider renting a villa with stunning coastal views.

- **Villa Treville (Positano)**
  - **Why Stay Here:** This luxury villa offers individually designed suites, lush gardens, and private terraces with panoramic views of Positano.
  - Cost: From €1,500 per night.
  - Facilities:Private dining, exclusive beach access, and personal butler service.
  - Website: Villa Treville
- **Villa Cimbrone (Ravello)**
  - **Why Stay Here:** A historic villa with beautiful gardens, luxurious rooms, and one of the best viewpoints on the coast.
  - Cost: From €350 per night.
  - Facilities: Rooftop dining, infinity pool, and garden access.

- o **Website:** Villa Cimbrone

3. Cozy B&Bs and Family-Run Stays

For a warm, personalized experience, opt for a bed-and-breakfast or a family-run guesthouse.

- **Villa Rosa (Positano)**
  - o **Why Stay Here:** This charming B&B is just steps from Positano's main beach and offers spacious rooms with private balconies.
  - o **Cost:** From €180 per night.
  - o **Facilities:** Breakfast included, friendly hosts, and stunning views.
  - o **Website:** Villa Rosa
- **B&B Ravello Rooms (Ravello)**
  - o **Why Stay Here:** This affordable yet charming B&B is located just outside Ravello's main square, offering peaceful surroundings and great hospitality.
  - o **Cost:** From €120 per night.
  - o **Facilities:** Breakfast on the terrace, free parking, and personalized recommendations.
  - o **Website:** B&B Ravello Rooms
- **Miramalfi (Amalfi)**
  - o **Why Stay Here:**This family-run property offers cozy rooms with sea views and easy access to the center of Amalfi.
  - o **Cost:** From €150 per night.
  - o **Facilities:**Private beach access and a traditional restaurant.
  - o **Website:** Miramalfi

4. Budget-Friendly Options

Traveling on a budget doesn't mean missing out on the Amalfi Coast's charm. Here are some wallet-friendly options:

- **Hostel Brikette (Positano)**
  - <u>Why Stay Here:</u> Ideal for solo travelers and backpackers, this hostel offers dormitory-style accommodations with incredible views.
  - <u>Cost:</u> From €40 per night.
  - <u>Facilities:</u> Shared kitchen, terrace, and social events.
- **Agriturismo Orrido di Pino (Agerola)**
  - <u>Why Stay Here:</u>This farm stay combines rustic charm with delicious homemade meals using locally sourced ingredients.
  - <u>Cost:</u> From €70 per night.
  - <u>Facilities:</u>Free breakfast, farm tours, and a peaceful setting.
- **Camping Beata Solitudo (Agerola)**
  - <u>Why Stay Here:</u> Perfect for nature lovers, this campsite offers tent pitches, bungalows, and affordable accommodations with easy access to hiking trails.
  - <u>Cost:</u> From €25 per night.

Chapter 7: Day Trips

The Naples and Amalfi Coast region is perfectly situated for unforgettable day trips to nearby islands and historical landmarks.Here are the top destinations you should consider for your day trips.

A.Capri

Why Visit:
Capri is synonymous with glamour, beauty, and relaxation. Its dramatic cliffs, turquoise waters, and elegant shops make it one of the most iconic islands in the world.

How to Get There:

- Take a ferry from Naples (50 minutes) or Sorrento (25 minutes). Ferries cost €20–€25 each way.
- Fast ferries operate frequently, especially during peak season (May–September).

What to Do:

- **Blue Grotto (Grotta Azzurra):** Take a boat tour to this magical sea cave, where sunlight creates an otherworldly blue glow. Entry costs €14 plus the boat fee.
- **Monte Solaro:** Take the chairlift from Anacapri to the island's highest point for panoramic views of the Bay of Naples and Amalfi Coast. Round-trip tickets cost €12.
- **Piazzetta di Capri:** Relax with a coffee in the island's bustling square, often referred to as "the world's living room."

Where to Eat:

- **Ristorante Il Geranio:** Overlooking the Faraglioni Rocks, this restaurant offers fresh seafood and elegant dishes.

Best Time to Visit:
Spring and early autumn for mild weather and fewer crowds.

B. Procida

Why Visit:
Less touristy than Capri, Procida is a charming island with colorful houses, quiet beaches, and authentic Italian vibes. Its recent stint as Italy's Capital of Culture has added to its allure.

How to Get There:

- Ferries from Naples take about 40 minutes. Tickets cost €15–€20 each way.

What to Do:

- **Marina Corricella:** Stroll along the island's picturesque fishing village, lined with pastel-colored houses and traditional boats.
- **Terra Murata:** Visit this historic hilltop village, home to the Abbey of San Michele and breathtaking views.
- **Beaches:** Relax at Chiaiolella Beach, a peaceful spot with crystal-clear waters.

Where to Eat:

- **La Lampara:** A local favorite offering fresh seafood and stunning harbor views.

Best Time to Visit:
Spring and summer for the best weather and vibrant island life.

C.Ischia

Why Visit:
Known as the "Green Island," Ischia is famous for its natural thermal springs, lush landscapes, and sandy beaches. It's a perfect retreat for relaxation and wellness.

How to Get There:

- Ferries from Naples take 60–90 minutes. Tickets cost €15–€25 each way.

What to Do:

- **Poseidon Thermal Gardens:** Spend a rejuvenating day at this luxurious thermal spa, with pools set amidst tropical gardens. Entry costs €35–€50.

- **Aragonese Castle:** Explore this historic fortress perched on a volcanic rock connected to the island by a causeway. Entry costs €12.
- **Sant'Angelo:** Discover this charming car-free village, ideal for strolling and relaxing by the sea.

Where to Eat:

- **Da Ciccio:** A family-run restaurant serving traditional Ischian cuisine, including rabbit stew (*coniglio all'ischitana*).

Best Time to Visit:
Late spring to early autumn, when the thermal spas and beaches are at their best.

D.Pompeii

Why Visit:
Pompeii is a UNESCO World Heritage Site that offers an extraordinary glimpse into life in an ancient Roman city, preserved by the eruption of Mount Vesuvius in 79 AD.

How to Get There:

- Take the Circumvesuviana train from Naples (35 minutes). Tickets cost €3.60 each way.

What to Do:

- **Forum:** Explore the heart of Pompeii's political and social life.

- **Villa of the Mysteries:** Marvel at the well-preserved frescoes depicting mysterious rituals.
- **Amphitheater:** Visit one of the oldest surviving Roman amphitheaters.

Where to Eat:

- Nearby restaurants like **Hortus Pompeii** offer a mix of Italian classics and quick bites for tourists.

Cost:
Entry to Pompeii costs €16. Guided tours start at €30.

Best Time to Visit:
Spring or autumn to avoid the summer heat.

E.Mount Vesuvius

Why Visit:
A hike to the summit of Mount Vesuvius offers breathtaking views and a chance to peer into the crater of one of the world's most famous volcanoes.

How to Get There:

- From Pompeii, take a shuttle bus to the Vesuvius National Park entrance. Round-trip tickets cost about €20.

What to Do:

- **Hike to the Summit:** The 30-minute hike is moderately challenging but worth it for the views.

- **Explore the Crater:** Learn about the volcano's history and geology from guides stationed at the top.

Cost:
Entry to the park costs €10.

Best Time to Visit:
Spring and autumn for cooler weather and clear skies.

Chapter 8: Itinerary Planning

A. 3-Day Itinerary

<u>Day 1: Exploring Naples</u>

- **Morning:**
  - Visit the **Naples National Archaeological Museum** to see treasures from Pompeii and Herculaneum.
  - Stroll through **Spaccanapoli**, the narrow street that cuts through Naples' historic center.
- **Lunch:** Enjoy authentic Neapolitan pizza at **L'Antica Pizzeria da Michele**.
- **Afternoon:**
  - Tour **Naples Underground** (*Napoli Sotterranea*).
  - Stop by **Piazza del Plebiscito** and **Galleria Umberto I**.

- **Evening:**
  - Dine along the Lungomare promenade with a view of Mount Vesuvius.

Day 2: Pompeii and Mount Vesuvius

- **Morning:**
  - Take the Circumvesuviana train to **Pompeii** and explore the ancient ruins.
- **Lunch:** Grab a quick bite near the site.
- **Afternoon:**
  - Hike to the crater of **Mount Vesuvius** for stunning views.
- **Evening:** Return to Naples for dinner at **Trattoria Nennella**, a local favorite.

Day 3: Capri

- **Morning:**
  - Take a ferry to **Capri**. Visit the **Blue Grotto** and enjoy a chairlift ride to **Monte Solaro** in Anacapri.
- **Lunch:** Dine in Capri town with views of the Faraglioni Rocks.
- **Afternoon:**
  - Stroll through the **Gardens of Augustus** and shop in boutique stores.
- **Evening:** Return to Naples or stay in Capri for a luxurious overnight experience.

B.7-Day Itinerary

Day 1: Arrival in Naples

- Explore the city's historic center and enjoy its vibrant food scene.

Day 2: Pompeii and Herculaneum

- Visit **Pompeii** in the morning and **Herculaneum** in the afternoon.

Day 3: Capri

- Spend a full day exploring **Capri** as described above.

Day 4: Positano

- Travel to the Amalfi Coast and base yourself in **Positano**.
- Relax on the beach and explore the charming streets.

Day 5: Amalfi and Ravello

- Visit **Amalfi Cathedral**, then head to **Ravello** to see **Villa Rufolo** and **Villa Cimbrone**.

Day 6: Path of the Gods and Praiano

- Hike the **Path of the Gods** in the morning. Spend the afternoon relaxing in **Praiano**, a quieter village.

Day 7: Departure

- Enjoy a leisurely morning and depart for your next destination.

C. Tailoring Your Trip

Your journey to Naples and the Amalfi Coast can be personalized to fit your interests and travel style.

1. **Romantic Escape:**
   - Stay in luxury hotels like **Le Sirenuse** or **Belmond Hotel Caruso.**
   - Include fine dining experiences and private boat tours.
2. **Family-Friendly Vacation:**
   - Base in Naples or Sorrento for easy access to attractions.
   - Visit Pompeii, take a ferry to Procida, and enjoy the beaches.
3. **Adventure Seekers:**
   - Focus on hiking (e.g., **Path of the Gods**) and water sports like kayaking or snorkeling.
4. **Budget Travelers:**
   - Stay in hostels or budget B&Bs.
   - Use public transportation and dine at local trattorias.

Chapter 9: Local Cuisine and Wine

The Naples and Amalfi Coast region is a food lover's paradise, with every meal offering a glimpse into the region's soul.

A.Best Restaurants and Food Markets

Top Restaurants in Naples

1. **L'Antica Pizzeria da Michele**
   - **Why Go:** Known as the birthplace of authentic Neapolitan pizza, this iconic spot has been delighting diners since 1870. The menu is simple: choose between Margherita and Marinara pizzas, each crafted to perfection.
   - **Location:** Via Cesare Sersale 1, Naples.
   - **Cost:** Around €6 for a whole pizza.

- **Pro Tip:** Arrive early or expect a queue; it's worth the wait!

2. **Trattoria Nennella**
   - **Why Go:** Located in the vibrant Quartieri Spagnoli, this bustling trattoria serves hearty, affordable Neapolitan classics like *pasta e patate con provola e ragù alla Napoletana.*
   - **Location:** Vico Lungo Teatro Nuovo 103, Naples.
   - **Cost:** Main courses from €10.
3. **La Masardona**
   - **Why Go:** For the best *pizza fritta* (fried pizza) in Naples, head to this local favorite. It's a must-try, indulgent street food experience.
   - **Location:** Via Giulio Cesare Capaccio 27, Naples.
   - **Cost:** From €8 per pizza.

Top Restaurants on the Amalfi Coast

1. **Chez Black (Positano)**
   - **Why Go:** With a prime beachfront location, this iconic restaurant serves fresh seafood and Italian classics. Its lively atmosphere and romantic setting make it a favorite.
   - **Location:** Via del Brigantino 19, Positano.
   - **Cost:** Starters from €15, main courses from €25.
2. **Trattoria da Gemma (Amalfi)**
   - **Why Go:** A family-run restaurant offering authentic Amalfi flavors, such

as *scialatielli ai frutti di mare* and *torta al limone*.

- ○ **Location:** Via Fra' Gerardo Sasso 11, Amalfi.
- ○ **Cost:** Main courses from €20.

3. **La Tagliata (Positano)**
   - ○ **Why Go:** Perched high above Positano, this farm-to-table restaurant offers a fixed menu of freshly made pasta, grilled meats, and local vegetables. The panoramic views are breathtaking.
   - ○ **Location:** Via Monsignor Vito Talamo 17, Positano.
   - ○ **Cost:** Around €40 per person for a full meal.

Best Food Markets in Naples

1. **Pignasecca Market**
   - ○ **Why Go:** This bustling market is a sensory overload of fresh seafood, seasonal produce, and street food. It's a must for sampling local life.
   - ○ **Location:** Near Via Toledo, Naples.
   - ○ **Pro Tip:** Try the fried seafood cones (*cuoppo di mare fritto*) from one of the vendors.
2. **Mercato di Porta Nolana**
   - ○ **Why Go:** A seafood lover's dream, this market is where locals buy the freshest catch of the day. You'll also find fruits, vegetables, and spices.
   - ○ **Location:** Piazza Nolana, Naples.
3. **Mercato dell'Antignano**
   - ○ **Why Go:** A local gem in the Vomero district, this market offers everything

from cheeses and cured meats to homemade pasta.
  o **Location:** Piazza Antignano, Naples.

Best Food Markets on the Amalfi Coast

1. **Minori Food Market**
   o **Why Go:** A small, local market offering fresh lemons, mozzarella, and other Amalfi Coast staples.
   o **Pro Tip:** Pick up some locally made limoncello as a souvenir.
2. **Ravello Farmers' Market**
   o **Why Go:** Located in the town square, this market features fresh produce, flowers, and handmade crafts.
3. **Conca dei Marini Weekly Market**
   o **Why Go:** A quiet market with a mix of fresh food, clothing, and household items.

Pro Tips for Dining and Markets

1. **Timing Matters:**
   o Restaurants typically open for lunch from 12:30 PM to 3:00 PM and for dinner from 7:30 PM to 10:30 PM.
   o Markets are best visited early in the morning for the freshest produce and seafood.
2. **Reserve Ahead:**
   o Popular spots like Chez Black and L'Antica Pizzeria da Michele fill up quickly, so reservations are recommended where possible.
3. **Cash:**

o Many markets and small trattorias only accept cash, so carry euros with you.

B.Wine and Lemon Liqueurs of the Region

1. Falanghina (White Wine)

- **Flavor Profile:** Crisp and fruity, with notes of citrus, green apple, and floral undertones.
- **Best Paired With:** Seafood dishes, especially *linguine alle vongole* (linguine with clams).
- **Where to Taste:**
  o **Feudi di San Gregorio Winery (Avellino):** Known for its high-quality Falanghina.
  o **Local Restaurants:** Many Amalfi Coast restaurants serve this versatile wine.

2. Greco di Tufo (White Wine)

- **Flavor Profile:** Full-bodied and aromatic, with hints of peach, almond, and a minerally finish.
- **Best Paired With:** Grilled fish, creamy pasta dishes, or Caprese salad.
- **Where to Taste:**
  o **Cantina del Taburno (Benevento):** A great stop for wine enthusiasts exploring Campania.

3. Aglianico (Red Wine)

- **Flavor Profile:** Bold and tannic, with notes of black cherry, plum, and earthy spices. Often referred to as "the Barolo of the South."

- **Best Paired With:** Rich meats, such as lamb or *ragù alla Napoletana.*
- **Where to Taste:**
  - **Mastroberardino Winery (Avellino):** One of the most prestigious producers of Aglianico.
  - **Local Enotecas (Wine Bars):** Look for small, family-run establishments in Naples or Ravello.

Limoncello

What It Is:
Limoncello is a sweet and tangy liqueur made from the peels of *sfusato amalfitano*, the Amalfi Coast's giant, fragrant lemons. The process involves steeping lemon peels in alcohol and mixing the infusion with sugar and water to create a refreshing digestif.

Where to Try:

1. **Antichi Sapori d'Amalfi (Amalfi):** A renowned producer offering tastings and tours.
2. **Limoncello di Capri (Capri):** One of the oldest limoncello brands, with a charming shop on the island.

How to Enjoy:

- Serve chilled in a small glass after a meal.
- Drizzle it over desserts like gelato or use it in cocktails.

Cost:
A bottle of locally made limoncello costs around €10–€20, depending on the producer.

Unique Liqueurs and Spirits

1. **Finocchietto:**
   - A fennel liqueur with a sweet, herbal flavor, often served after meals.
2. **Meloncello:**
   - A creamy variation of limoncello made with cantaloupe or honeydew melon.
3. **Nocillo:**
   - A walnut liqueur with warm, spiced notes, typically enjoyed during winter.

Where to Buy:
Visit specialty shops in Amalfi, Ravello, or Naples for authentic products made by local artisans.

Wine and Limoncello Tours

For a deeper dive into the region's wine and liqueur-making traditions, consider booking a tour.

1. **Vineyard Tours:**
   - **Marisa Cuomo Winery (Furore):** Nestled in the cliffs, this winery offers tastings of its award-winning Costa d'Amalfi DOC wines. Tours start at €40 per person.
   - **Tenuta San Francesco (Tramonti):** Explore a family-run vineyard producing organic wines.
2. **Limoncello Factory Visits:**
   - **Il Gusto della Costa (Praiano):** Learn the art of limoncello-making and sample various citrus liqueurs.
   - **L'Alambicco (Sorrento):** A small-scale producer offering intimate tours.

How to Book:

- Use platforms like GetYourGuide or Viator to book tours in advance.
- Many producers also allow walk-ins but call ahead during peak seasons.

Tips for Enjoying Local Drinks

1. **Ask for Local Pairings:**
   - Many restaurants and enotecas offer wine pairings with their dishes for a full sensory experience.
2. **Take Home a Souvenir:**
   - Bottles of limoncello, Greco di Tufo, or Aglianico make excellent gifts or keepsakes.
3. **Savor, Don't Rush:**
   - Both wine and limoncello are best enjoyed slowly. Take your time to appreciate the craftsmanship in each sip.

Chapter 10: Shopping and Souvenirs

A. What to Buy in Naples and the Amalfi Coast

1. Ceramics: Handcrafted Masterpieces

Why It's Special:
The Amalfi Coast is famous for its brightly colored, hand-painted ceramics. These pieces often feature traditional designs inspired by the region's lemons, coastal scenery, and floral patterns.

What to Buy:

- **Plates and Bowls:** Perfect for adding a Mediterranean flair to your dining table.
- **Vases and Decorative Tiles:** Beautiful for home décor.
- **Ceramic Lemons:** Small decorative items that capture the essence of Amalfi.

<u>Where to Shop:</u>

1. **Ceramiche Casola (Positano):** Renowned for its exquisite hand-painted dinnerware and custom designs.
2. **Ceramiche D'Arte Carmela (Ravello):** A family-run shop specializing in vibrant ceramics made with traditional techniques.
3. **Vietri sul Mare:** This coastal village is the hub of ceramic production in the region, with dozens of artisan workshops.

<u>Pro Tip:</u>
If you're worried about transporting fragile items, many shops offer international shipping services.

2. Limoncello and Lemon-Themed Products

<u>Why It's Special:</u>
The Amalfi Coast's *sfusato amalfitano* lemons are world-famous for their fragrance and sweetness, making limoncello and lemon-themed items the perfect souvenirs.

<u>What to Buy:</u>

- **Limoncello:** A sweet lemon liqueur that's an iconic taste of the region.
- **Candied Lemon Peels:** A delightful snack or gift.

- **Lemon Soap and Perfumes:** Luxurious, citrus-scented bath products.

<u>Where to Shop:</u>

1. **Antichi Sapori d'Amalfi (Amalfi):** A top spot for authentic limoncello and other lemon-based products.
2. **Limonoro (Sorrento):** Known for its high-quality limoncello and gourmet lemon treats.

<u>Pro Tip:</u>
Look for small-batch, locally made limoncello to ensure the best quality.

3. Leather Goods

<u>Why It's Special:</u>
Naples has a long tradition of leather craftsmanship, producing high-quality shoes, handbags, and accessories.

<u>What to Buy:</u>

- **Handmade Sandals:** Particularly popular in Positano, where artisans craft custom sandals to fit your feet.
- **Leather Bags and Wallets:** Stylish and durable souvenirs.

<u>Where to Shop:</u>

1. **Safari Sandals (Positano):** Known for bespoke leather sandals crafted while you wait.
2. **Marinella (Naples):** Famous for luxurious ties, leather goods, and men's accessories.

4. Artisanal Food Products

Why It's Special:
The culinary traditions of Naples and the Amalfi Coast are reflected in their artisanal food products, which make excellent gifts or indulgences for yourself.

What to Buy:

- **Pasta:** Handmade or dried pasta in unique shapes like *scialatielli*.
- **Olive Oil:** Extra virgin olive oil infused with local herbs or lemon.
- **Cheese:** Aged pecorino, buffalo mozzarella, or *provolone del monaco*.
- **Sweets:** *Sfogliatelle, babà al rum*, or jars of marmalade made from local fruit.

Where to Shop:

1. **Pignasecca Market (Naples):** A lively market where you can find fresh and packaged local specialties.
2. **Minori Food Market (Minori):** Ideal for stocking up on jams, marmalades, and other gourmet items.

5. Coral and Cameos

Why It's Special:
The Gulf of Naples is famous for its coral jewelry and intricately carved cameos, which have been crafted here for centuries.

What to Buy:

- **Coral Necklaces and Bracelets:** Made with locally sourced coral.
- **Cameos:** Hand-carved from shells or coral, depicting mythological and floral designs.

<u>Where to Shop:</u>

1. **Ascione (Naples):** A historic jewelry store specializing in coral and cameos.
2. **Ravello Cameos (Ravello):** Known for its intricate, handcrafted designs.

<u>Pro Tip:</u>
Always ask for a certificate of authenticity when purchasing coral or cameos.

6. Nativity Figurines (Presepi)

<u>Why It's Special:</u>
Naples is world-famous for its elaborate nativity scenes (*presepi*), a tradition dating back to the 18th century.

<u>What to Buy:</u>

- **Handcrafted Figurines:** Ranging from holy figures to comical characters.
- **Miniature Accessories:** Tiny market stalls, fountains, and animals to enhance your nativity scene.

<u>Where to Shop:</u>

1. **Via San Gregorio Armeno (Naples):** This street is lined with artisan shops dedicated to nativity figurines and accessories.

7. Local Artwork and Prints

<u>Why It's Special:</u>
The stunning landscapes of the Amalfi Coast have inspired artists for generations, and you can take home a piece of that beauty.

<u>What to Buy:</u>

- **Watercolor Paintings:** Depicting coastal villages and seascapes.
- **Photography Prints:** High-quality prints of iconic Amalfi Coast views.

<u>Where to Shop:</u>

1. **Art Galleries in Positano and Ravello:** Many local artists sell their work directly from their studios.
2. **Street Vendors:** You'll find talented artists selling their pieces in piazzas and along promenades.

<u>**Tips for Shopping in Naples and the Amalfi Coast**</u>

1. **Haggle Respectfully:** In markets, bargaining is often expected, but always be polite.
2. **Carry Cash:** Smaller shops and market vendors may not accept cards.
3. **Check Shipping Options:** For larger or fragile items like ceramics, many shops offer international shipping.
4. **Buy Authentic:** Avoid mass-produced items; look for locally made goods to support artisans and ensure quality.

Conclusion

As we approach the final pages of the Naples and Amalfi Coast Travel Guide 2025, I want to thank you for allowing this guide to be your trusted companion on your journey through one of Italy's most enchanting regions. Together, we've explored the timeless charm of Naples, wandered along the breathtaking Amalfi Coast, and uncovered a world where history, culture, and natural beauty intertwine in perfect harmony.

Through these chapters, we've strolled through the streets of Naples, where every corner tells a story, and every meal is a celebration. We've marveled at the ancient ruins of Pompeii and felt the echoes of a civilization long past. Along the Amalfi Coast, we've admired pastel-hued villages clinging to cliffs, sailed across sparkling turquoise waters, and basked in the warm embrace of the Mediterranean sun. Along the way, I hope this guide has not only provided you with practical advice but also deepened your appreciation for the spirit and soul of this extraordinary destination.

Naples and the Amalfi Coast are more than places—they're experiences. They're the joy of sharing laughter over a perfect Margherita pizza in a Neapolitan piazza. They're the quiet wonder of gazing out at the endless blue of the Tyrrhenian Sea from Ravello's gardens. They're the thrill of winding along coastal roads, where every turn reveals a view more breathtaking than the last. These are moments that stay with you, moments that remind us why we travel—to feel alive, connected, and inspired.

As you set out on your journey, I encourage you to embrace the essence of this region. Relish the vibrant energy of Naples, savor the slow rhythms of life along the Amalfi Coast, and let curiosity guide you. Some of the most unforgettable memories come from the unexpected—a hidden trattoria tucked down an alley, a sunset viewed from a secluded terrace, or the kindness of a local sharing their favorite spot.

Thank you for choosing the Naples and Amalfi Coast Travel Guide 2025 to be part of your adventure. My hope is that it has not only helped you plan your trip but also inspired you to experience this region with open eyes, a full heart, and a willingness to be surprised by its magic.

May your time in Naples and along the Amalfi Coast be as vibrant, serene, and unforgettable as these places themselves. And who knows? Perhaps one day, our paths will cross again—on a bustling street in Naples, on a boat gliding across the sea, or in the golden light of an Amalfi Coast sunset. Until then, happy exploring!

Bonus Chapter: Recipes

1. Pizza Margherita (Naples)

Ingredients:

- 500g (4 cups) all-purpose flour
- 325ml (1 1/3 cups) water
- 10g (2 tsp) salt
- 3g (1 tsp) dry yeast
- 250g (1 cup) San Marzano tomatoes, crushed
- 200g (1 cup) fresh mozzarella, sliced
- Fresh basil leaves
- Extra virgin olive oil

Preparation Steps:

1. **Prepare the Dough:**

   - Mix flour, water, salt, and yeast in a bowl. Knead until smooth and elastic.
   - Cover and let rise for 2–3 hours until doubled in size.
2. **Prepare the Toppings:**

   - Crush San Marzano tomatoes and season with a pinch of salt.
3. **Shape the Dough:**

   - Divide the dough into four portions. Roll each into a circle about 10 inches wide.

4. **Assemble the Pizza:**

   o Spread tomato sauce evenly on each base. Add mozzarella slices and fresh basil leaves. Drizzle with olive oil.

5. **Bake:**

   o Preheat your oven to 500°F (260°C) with a pizza stone or baking sheet inside. Bake pizzas for 7–9 minutes until the crust is golden and crisp.

2. Spaghetti alle Vongole (Amalfi Coast)

Ingredients:

- 400g (14 oz) spaghetti
- 1kg (2.2 lbs) fresh clams
- 3 garlic cloves, minced
- 4 tbsp extra virgin olive oil
- 1/2 cup dry white wine
- Fresh parsley, chopped
- Salt and red pepper flakes (optional)

Preparation Steps:

1. **Clean the Clams:**

   o Soak the clams in salted water for 30 minutes to remove sand. Rinse thoroughly.

2. **Cook the Spaghetti:**

   o Boil spaghetti in salted water until al dente. Reserve 1 cup of pasta water.

3. **Prepare the Sauce:**

o Heat olive oil in a large skillet. Sauté garlic until fragrant.

o Add clams and wine, cover, and cook for 5 minutes until the clams open. Discard any that remain closed.

4. **Combine:**

o Add spaghetti to the skillet with clams. Toss with parsley and reserved pasta water for a creamy finish.

5. **Serve:**

o Plate immediately and garnish with additional parsley.

3. Delizia al Limone (Lemon Delight)

Ingredients for Sponge Cake:

- 3 eggs
- 100g (1/2 cup) sugar
- 75g (2/3 cup) flour
- 25g (1/4 cup) cornstarch

Ingredients for Lemon Cream:

- 200ml (3/4 cup) milk
- 2 egg yolks
- 50g (1/4 cup) sugar
- 1 tbsp cornstarch
- Juice and zest of 2 lemons

Preparation Steps:

1. **Make the Sponge Cake:**

- o Whisk eggs and sugar until fluffy. Gently fold in flour and cornstarch.
- o Bake at 350°F (175°C) in a greased pan for 20 minutes. Cool and cut into dome shapes.

2. **Make the Lemon Cream:**

- o Heat milk in a saucepan. Whisk egg yolks, sugar, and cornstarch in a bowl, then add lemon juice and zest.
- o Slowly mix hot milk into the egg mixture, then return to the pan and cook until thickened.

3. **Assemble:**

- o Fill the sponge cakes with lemon cream and glaze the tops with more cream. Refrigerate until chilled.

4. Scialatielli ai Frutti di Mare (Seafood Pasta)

Ingredients:

- 400g (14 oz) scialatielli pasta (or fresh tagliatelle)
- 500g (1.1 lbs) mixed seafood (clams, mussels, squid, shrimp)
- 3 garlic cloves, minced
- 4 tbsp extra virgin olive oil
- 1/2 cup dry white wine
- 1 can cherry tomatoes
- Fresh parsley, chopped

Preparation Steps:

1. **Clean the Seafood:**

- Rinse clams and mussels; slice squid into rings and peel shrimp.

2. **Prepare the Sauce:**

   - Heat olive oil in a large pan. Sauté garlic and add cherry tomatoes. Cook for 5 minutes.
   - Add seafood and wine, cover, and cook until clams and mussels open.

3. **Cook the Pasta:**

   - Boil scialatielli in salted water until al dente.

4. **Combine:**

   - Toss the pasta in the seafood sauce. Sprinkle with parsley before serving.

5. Sfogliatella (Neapolitan Pastry)

Ingredients:

- 250g (2 cups) all-purpose flour
- 100g (1/2 cup) sugar
- 100g (1/2 cup) ricotta cheese
- 50g (1/4 cup) semolina
- 2 tbsp candied orange peel, chopped
- 1 tsp cinnamon
- Butter (for dough layers)

Preparation Steps:

1. **Prepare the Dough:**

   - Mix flour and water into a dough. Roll thinly and brush with melted butter. Fold and chill multiple times to create layers.

2. **Make the Filling:**

   o Cook semolina in water until thick. Mix with ricotta, sugar, candied orange peel, and cinnamon.

3. **Assemble:**

   o Roll out dough, cut into circles, and fill with the ricotta mixture. Fold and seal.

4. **Bake:**

   o Bake at 375°F (190°C) for 20–25 minutes until golden. Dust with powdered sugar.

Tips:

1. **Use Fresh Ingredients:** The quality of local produce and seafood is essential to recreate authentic flavors.
2. **Be Patient:** Many traditional recipes require time and attention to detail.
3. **Pair with Local Wines:** Enjoy these dishes with regional wines like Falanghina or Aglianico for a complete experience.

Made in the USA
Monee, IL
11 May 2025